MW01286654

Praise for Florida Water

"This is aja monet at her most lucid and vulnerable, offering an intimate portrait in love, drowning in it, and kissing us each time she comes up for air. The politics of love and memory betrothed to a poet's passion to touch and be touched by perspective—and in real ways—she holds herself in her own arms, yet somehow we, all our loved ones and blessed ancestors, fit in her embrace. Here is where maturity and grace never forgets to remind us of its edge, its pain, and unanswered questions—where a moment in time finds its timelessness. Here is a poet ripening beyond her bruises, clear-eyed and lovingly, sprinkling holy water on angels and demons alike."

—Saul Williams

"aja monet always opens the portal. . . . Read her work and prepare to time travel into the possibilities of your own heart and our beloved community."

—Alexis Pauline Gumbs

"The stewards of this land and the Africans dragged here tell us water is life. Channeling ancestral wisdom, aja monet shows us water is also love, power, reflection, blue(s), bodies. Water heals, cleanses, blesses; it gives life and can take it away. Water is older than history and yet never forgets. aja monet's poems are water, and these poems were born at the crossroads of the world, where Turtle Island meets the Caribbean Sea. In this death-dealing world, *Florida Water* will quench our collective thirst for living."

—Robin D. G. Kelley

"aja monet is a poet's poet. She uses the language like a painter. . . . Her love and grief for humanity is paramount. Her hopes and dreams are for a better world."

—Abiodun Oyewole

Praise for
My Mother Was
a Freedom Fighter

"aja monet's poetry offers us textures of feeling and radical shifts of meaning that expand our capacity to envision and fight for new worlds. From Brooklyn, USA to Hebron, Occupied Palestine, we take a feminist journey through rage and serenity, through violence and love, through ancient times and imagined futures. This stunning volume reminds us that conflict and contradiction can produce hope and that poetry can orient us toward a future we may not yet realize we want."

—Angela Y. Davis

"We who follow the dynamic poetry of aja monet know her to be a wizard of optimism and musicality. *My Mother Was a Freedom Fighter* reminds us of her wisdom. These poems are made of the black woman genius they praise: 'the ghost of women once girls,' 'mothers who did the best they could,' and 'daughters of a new day.' monet is a child of old school black power and a daughter of the myriad political traumas of today. Her poetry is indispensable. These poems are fire."

—Terrance Hayes

Florida Water

poems

aja monet

© 2025 aja monet

Published in 2025 by
Haymarket Books
P.O. Box 180165
Chicago, IL 60618
773-583-7884
www.haymarketbooks.org
info@haymarketbooks.org

ISBN: 978-164259-967-1

Distributed to the trade in the US through Consortium Book Sales and
Distribution (www.cbsd.com) and internationally through Ingram Publisher
Services International (www.ingramcontent.com).

This book was published with the generous support of Lannan Foundation,
Marguerite Casey Foundation, and Wallace Action Fund.

Special discounts are available for bulk purchases by organizations and
institutions. Please email info@haymarketbooks.org for more information.

Cover photograph by Meg Turner.
Cover design by Rachel Cohen.

Printed in the United States.

Library of Congress Cataloging-in-Publication data is available.

10 9 8 7 6 5 4 3 2 1

for my grandmother Graciela Bacquie

and all the parts of you i love in me

thank you for teaching me how to read and bathe a spirit

in memory of my brothers

Daniel Agnew & Chad Gittens

Two things everybody's got tuh do fuh theyselves. They got tuh go tuh God, and they got tuh find out about livin' fuh theyselves.

—Zora Neale Hurston's Janie, from Their Eyes Were Watching God

There are memories between us

deeper than grief

—Keorapetse Kgositsile, from "The Elegance of Memory"

Sometimes I fall in love.

Sometimes it falls on me.

And it's heavy.

—SHENZI, from "Us"

Are you sure, sweetheart, that you want to be well?

—Toni Cade Bambara's Minnie Ransom, from The Salt Eaters

contents

initiation 1

my first memory was drowning 5

the water is rising 7

florida water 25

the foreshadowing furlough 27

highs and lows 29

yemaya 31

the perfect storm 33

choice 36

the porch is a throne of small talk 37

if it would've went how it could've 38

a state of emergency 39

saltwater railroad 42

the absurdity of law 43

sign language 44

the fool 45

is love a commons? 46

wanted child, 48

hand wash only 49

frank, ocean 51

sanibel will always be ours 52

castaway 53

maroonage 56

smoke signals 58

angels waging sit-ins on a canvas 59

magician city 60

solidarity 61

for freedoms 62

for the kids who live 64

garner 67

in justice 70

her 74

it is worthy to give god praise 77

maroon poetry festival 80

i am celebrating a woman i love who loved me before 82

drizzling moonshine 87

daughters of the doorway 89

a poem for agnes furey 91

every media minute 92

national immigrant integration conference 95

the devil you know 97

a livable love 101

lotus flower 103

give yourself back to you 104

i am 105

when the sun goes down 107

from eternity to eternity 108

the living room 110

in the brooklyn of our being 114

life vest 116

what does it mean to be considered? 117

what a poem is 119

supreme love 122

say it with your chest 124

gratitude 127

initiation

i am devoted to the poetry of being alive. i want to do something about it. to try. to dream. to love. to envision. to struggle with people for the bettering of our being. to exist. and then to disappear. i search for community and discover to not belong is a kind of belonging. poetry isn't fixed on place or identity. poetry isn't concerned with perfection or political correctness. it demands our vulnerability. our will to change and be changed. poetry creates a cosmos for connection. it expands and extends our reach and just when you think you understand, you question the very pursuit of understanding.

organizing in movement spaces at times can be so rigid with indoctrination and rhetoric that we are rarely invited to bring our whole visible and invisible selves into the work. our curiosity. our fear. our insecurity. our poetry. we come to this work shaped by the culture we were raised in and if we want to change the nature of our systems we must examine our convictions. we must examine ourselves. no one can possibly hold you more accountable than you hold yourself. the poem can be a compassionate lens. a restorative process in good faith. a reckoning. a poem can rinse, reflect, and reveal us. i give thanks for the intimacy of cleansing poems. the living that brings a poem into being. the search for language and the acceptance of its limitations. some of the strongest poems written will never be published. they show up in our hearts like footsteps in the sand along the shore. there and then not.

moving to florida from new york city for love and community provided me with space to confront both the personal and political. to invite all aspects of my unself as lover, poet, and cultural worker. i learned to move between identities rather interchangeably. each one deepened the other. i feel most home in the flow between this and that, there and here, them and me, him and me. i was in relationship with a community organizer and we used our home as a gathering space for artists, organizers, and activists. i gave it my very all. i fell in love with the land, the air, the water. us and our people. it is difficult enough to endure loss or abuse whether it be by the state or by the people we love most intimately and yet to remain compassionate, soft, to seek deeper into the complexity of ourselves. to taste the salt of our sweat and tears and to not become stone. to not become that which was done to us. to not fall in love with our anger.

to be water. a body of water. to know thirst. to quench it. to prepare this bath of words rushing with nowhere to go. the ocean calling out through you. vast and everlasting. when there is a poem dripping out of the bathroom sink, oscillating from the ceiling fan in the bedroom, dew waving on leaves peering through the window. a kind of reading. when there is a hurricane of poems raging on the front yard. sneakers piled up at the screen door. i could not unsee beyond where we were as though there is a seeing without eyes felt in following each knowing as if it is already here. to arrive before leaving.

i made a home with someone and then it was unmade. i charted forward with the whole heart of myself and left precaution to dealings with tsa agents, police officers, or idf soldiers. i unbuttoned and unbuckled with will and want for a lover who was more than that though he treated me as less more often than id like to admit. but it was beautiful and revolutionary before it wasn't, like all true loves. and we made the movement our everything. and even when we gave our all it was never enough. and when we wanted to rest we fought and when we wanted to fight we cried and when we wanted to cry we laughed.

we were imprisoned by our desire to be free. it was the poets in Dade Correctional who revealed us to us. to be fugitive. what goes uncaptured. a meditation on maroonage. meaning neither mentor nor mentee. to be mirrored. the frustration of what was for the pursuit of what will be. a freeing between the lines. the murder of Darren Rainey by the State. water as weapon. water as wound and storyteller. water as distance as in between. as essence. the currents of feeling flowing rigorous as rivers alongside earth entrenched or entangled in the waiting room of waterfronts without walls or barricades. rushing through us. water as truthteller. listening to the land. the unfamiliar of us wandering. believe you me him and i met in Palestine overlooking a new endless scape of light and i was lit with a liquid flame, wet with the weight of rage. having seen the firsthand audacity of evil. only to return to the States more enraged. willing to die. choosing to live. in love with the wand of a body withering and weathering. sea levels rising and the choking tides of racism. you ever been who you was suppose to be? waterfalls and fresh water springs. soaked with grief. florida wet with blood. the blessing and battleground.

how writing a poem became a form of organizing or how organizing is a poetic form. how the page failed me. the courage and compass created in the process of struggle. the growth. to be transformed. poetry is the wading through or with, diving further. in depths. the why. the door to door blues of organizing in south florida. the paintbrush of canvassing in neighborhoods. the heart as puddle. to be shapeless as the swamp. we give thanks to the water spirits.

i was raised by the prescriptive baths of seers. the gospel of Florida Water. my grandmother would send us home with boiled herbs, perfumes, and agua florida shaken up in a retired two liter soda bottle with instructions to be obeyed by our bodies in a tub. i learned with eavesdropping eyes that seeing is a kind of listening. a reading is a rinse. the bath is a poem every spirit needs. this is an offering and an apology. for the years i did not know i was worth fighting or writing for. in the distant hinterland of self when i did not think i could go on i wrote and when i could not write i bathed. grief flooding the shaky floorboards of forever. the healing ritual of handwashing my heart in saltwater.

with these poems i am submerged. breathless breathing. to know tears is to become tears. is to fall and splash, smear and smudge. to absorb and melt to swallow and be swallowed. i come from a people of shallow breaths. i am not the voice of everywhere. i have particulars, pains, and premonitions. i do not speak for everyone though i love each person especially. i am not an organization or a voice for any people. i am a movement unto myself and i need to be loved just as i am loving. we ought to gaze at each other in awe as we do the stars. love, like poetry, is being submerged in water trying to grasp what can't be held. some of us develop fins. gills even. the ability to breathe with as opposed to against. to emerge both maroon and mermaid. a different kind of breathing and therein being. i honor the indigenous wisdom of florida and everything the water could teach me.

my first memory was drowning

i did not know i was drowning
at three years old, a toddler drifting
in a Florida swimming pool
amid the children's laughter
the squish of flip flops
the heaven of being lost
to be utterly ever all with
maybe on the other side of a memory
neglect is how i learn to fly
in a world of sink or swim
i float in the calm of chaos
riding the waves of bartered time
i melt into chlorine wrinkles of light
i choose to remember not knowing any better
a desire to play, to fall
free
i may have wept had i not been
surrounded by water
i forgot my lungs
the body was irrelevant
death was a twirl in the distance
an afterbirth
come close
there were no reflections or rearview mirrors
my name was a little shrine
a window into a whisper
the dead don't complain
i half-smiled at god
so this is how you do
what you do
near-life experience
when i came to
all the adults screaming
dry with suffering
i dripped from my mother's arms
tiny tears of the wide-eyed cosmos

offering no answers
i questioned breath
now i run to any body of water
let me swim

the water is rising

in other words
the water is rising
in the relic of rain

insects gossip about us
the dull huffing puffing of islands
the hush money howl of advertisements

electoral politics of greed
godless truths on the mouths of mountains
an inauguration for a growling earth

words caught in a wayward wing
the rage of rivers dressed as comrades

i walk with the runaways
in this there southern america

tomorrow's towering
thirst of a thousand yesterdays in our throats

the chokehold of change
the illiteracy of revolutionary lovers
on topsy-turvy tongues

emerging from the flames of homeland insecurity

still we move

all i know is dreamers drift through the threat of a door
an ambulance filled with books

in other words the water is rising

the difference between looking and seeing
crumbs of blood, a trail of tears

the only free people are prisoners of war
mapless belonging nowhere

the faith of forgetting
in the waiting hours, we go forward

a streetcar named surrender
money perishes in the face of the flood

enchanted by the question of existing at all
in other words, the water is rising

there's no such thing as home
everywhere is fleeing

we are the eye of the storm

in the absence of those we love, we listen
if ever we cannot learn from loss what it must teach

we will lose more even,
the gift of greater allegiances between us

in other words, the water is rising

                                   have you known longing to belong?

how the arms of ache reach for new heights of the heart
i climbed the freshwater rivers stumbling

rocks, stones, branches
i tightroped across bamboo

chasing waterfalls, i sought what saw me
courage startles the bruise
beaming in the dusty sun of what shines

be not fooled, there were showers
thunderous storms along the way

what we weather we within,
us today people of sun licked by all that glows
touched by the fingers of sky

those of us who know how to open the ocean door
like a chest of treasure upon the beating hum

we who can smell the weather
and taste the temperature of our sweat

we who tell the time of no time
the beauty of gestures
a ceremony of pain
mirror of maroons

in other words   the water is   r i s i n g

*

i edit the scab

wound to wound i navigate

honest walk of watering

to heal is to hurt

will i float or flop

i let go

i become a conduit

a rivulet

shapeless as a drop of dew

unfolding sea of secrets

this and that too shall pass

*

i dreamed a wave sent for me

my spirit, a suitcase
took off toward a luminous beam

a moon-stream lamenting droplets
a flame spilled on night, a well-lit street

curves of babbling earth
near the sea   all the same

i vanish immeasurable
i grow invisible

fields of electric emotion in evening air
a city sleeps, a song in a starved mouth

we come and go like a fist of dice
thrown at the horizon

little names stretched endless
in the palm of a hand

i rain
      dancing with the horn of high winds
ear hustling pitches of promises

i starve my stories   hazy

we set ourselves to the clock of sayings
we are everything we want and need

god
is a percussionist
his favorite instrument is the heart
without hesitation

this morning
i was thrown overboard
this evening i washed up ashore

traveling the distance of light
we are going to be alright
or so they say

we return to where we were
flowing, a forest
stars and moon are gateways

justice swift as an axe falls
a gentle flame in the sky
i laugh

the sea is a mother i embrace
all our voices are heard
at once the hurricane spares us

another shock doctrine
the sex of rain
the romance of trees

i discover a new tongue
tenses crowd the mouth

the earth meditates in shipwrecked kisses
    in this language there is no word for war
        nothing is legible

    w e   f l o o d

*

as beginning middle and end
to be fugitive and holding hands with the earth

in the waiting room of waterfronts
without walls or barricades

the unfamiliar of us wandering
washed up like plastic on a shoreline

to lose is to receive
to find is to be lost
to see is to revisit

where debts are not real
nor are receipts

manmade storms reveal us
i prepare this bath of words rushing
with nowhere to go

there are many kinds of heartbreak:
    the creaking kind
        cracks of light in corners
            crashing against cheek
      booming beating and brushing
    against the beach

inhale and exhale
knee deep in rain
a hunger for rage

i don't love you anymore rhythms
silent blinks spilling poems
for what was no longer is

wet memories pacing
floating futures
on cliffs and edges

    the forever of letting go

to be out of hands and within touch
the scorn of scars haunting lovers

    nowhere and nothing

the risk of answerless questions
the myth of meaning making

moonlight cussin' up a storm
the tender animal of my ears
worshipping the whooooosh of us

    a sea of secrets on a weighted tongue
dinner with the stars
paying the bill alone
sipping on survival

during a drought of dreams
the siren of storms
day-to-day climate change

the shortness of spring
winter overstaying her welcome

the hurricane's shoes at your front door
    knocking
        knocking
and then
    the great flood

*

there are days you are not who you try to be

put the phone down

go where it's quiet

in the bathroom

bathe with whispers

a shrine of self
of bluefunk

in the scat of steam
be naked

be stream of consciousness
be a live stream
a stream
    of yearning

rinsing and rustling
with deep down needs
ever reaching promises

be impatient with the you of your yous

the shower head is your lover

sing of wandering
of ways and whims

bathe in the blueness
of blessing the boat

soak and marvel at wrinkled skin
the passing of time

pages of people mope about
     self-care and sadness
          capitalism on steroids
               comparison drained spirits

there is a need for blues
when the weary don't know a way to go

toiling with day-to-day misery
blues make tears gleam
     grief by the reins

spared by a storm
dancing on drunk clouds with praying feet

the arms of thunder
waving in the smoke of sunlight

kissing the violet veins of wrists
the sex of trees sweating out their limbs

the utterances of leaves
drenched and whirring

                                        where every ache kneels?

the bliss of wind and tickled skin
a storm don't distinguish between rich and poor
but the recovery do

climate gentrification is
pissing on a graveyard
to the hurricane's relief

in the wing of thick heat
the sun's voice dripping
        wild humid music
roaring with the land
shedding trees toasting the sky

champagne tears flowing
people stare at change
through window blinds and mosquito screens

loose palms smacking the air
maroons muddied in the shade
of fleeing or far flung

*

ocean sprung
drowning in depths
wading through
what craves and swims within
to become the sea
i leave the shore
bathing in awe
moon-touched
looming over
mermaid flesh
cowrie eyes
in the echo chamber of shells

how we do what we do
is as important as why
context is the content
love or fear

from where do we work?

trust or threat?

what is your constitution?

are you showing up in the world or in your
work in a way that is sustainable for you
and your community?

most of us have an adversarial relationship with our body
we have pain, we want it to go away

have you listened to your body lately?

to be self-aware is to accept yourself as a self is not you
interrupt the pattern of your mind

do we want presence or absence?

when we express our thoughts too soon
we lose our agency
to listen
we learn to not learn
more concerned with being right than sincere
righteousness rather than presence
the fog of fury or regret
be compassionate with your silence
conflict is the highest form of intimacy
invite the world you want to see into your eyes
all safety is a place of risk
to be heartbroken is to see you're not sure what you're seeing
which way is up or down
you are a part of me that i do not yet know
keep your agreements

listen from the gut of your hands
                             can you locate yourself?
many move through the world looking for a threat
a cell can only vibrate as high as it's surroundings
i touched the fatigue of our love
only as strong as our ability to grieve together
imagine

                                        who is the one person you have not yet
                                        tried to love?

when we are absent from now we grieve the then
forgiveness is freedom from the war of when

*

rage is a sacred form / of self-care / and love is warrior sage / come to me
with all of you
bring me your boundaries

*

        whatever prevents people from taking action is   action. if we don't figure
        it out, nature will figure it out for us. nature is non-negotiable. if we don't
        talk about the moments we fought back the efforts to resist, we will forever
        go down in history as being complacent with our oppression, and there-
        in complicit in the oppression of others, we must always tell the stories
        of those who fought back and why what compels a person to anger or to
        radical love, they'll tell you militance is the story of soldiers intended
        to kill, and not of lovers intent on living, i feel for the grass that uproots
        pavement; nature is militant towards survival.

*

all i want is a porch swing

a rocking chair

a room to love in

a window to watch the days change

to spill between leaves

we are taught a history of misconceptions
distorted and partial truths
indifference is a deafening death

there's who i was before i knew myself
and there's the knowing
a spirit of discernment

to read people like books
with only beginnings and no ends
a body as braille, as vessel
truth is like cod-liver oil
        hard to taste

or swallow   a cleanse
i manifested in movement
shaking my womb of pulses

meditating in the whirl between here and there
this is the search for myself to be who i really am

a poem as a crown
or a vow
a blessing that endures
change as perpetual purging of what was and will be
the anguish of what is the same
she chose this life ready to love this bronze blemished body

listening for a calling in the calligraphy of her blood
she was a miracle taken for granted
the cosmic door between earth and all else

in the year beyond the year under a new waking day
shedding time like tears, we were there clinging to our elder's dreams

praying for the inconvenient courage to nourish and nurture
unfleshed truth to suck the meat off the bones of words
and to feed on the love of those who shouldered sadness

choose a name that makes them sit up straight
i have seen the mechanical elves
surrendered to the ego death

laughing and crying are the same calendar of emotions
the elves were mocking me
or the me i confused for us

characters contorting to shapes
yellow green black and white
little figures pushing strollers of feelings

      then there she was
      divine allness

she was the color of plants blushing or unfurling
neither beautiful nor plain
i felt myself die

a losing of all i held close
breathtaking and to breathe again
to be devoured and sifted through

to be reborn in a voice unsung
no longer mine if mine was even possible
a cascading tantrum of tears

i was a river and all rivers were like me
drenched in drifting

i was a womb and i was in a womb
and i was every womb there ever was
purple red deep indigo then fuchsia

i could see a voice
the sound i wanted to sing

i became all
all is as it will be
all is all and everything is nothing is something

                    who said i was born the first time?
                    why again?
language is a look over the edge
i am a runaway sentence, still running

beyond it there's no return
i could not unsee what i saw
nor unlisten to what i heard

i am made of the kiss that keeps on kissing
my body is a music lesson

i am the salutation
this is my solo before the curtains close and they bury me

i became the earth before and i will again
let them tell it she went sweet drunk on the flask of her own heart
beat, a folk song dripping from her chin

where the air is church and breath is deliverance
this is how beauty is made
more faithful than flesh

i live for the awe of my own dimples
discovering the corners of my smile
soft as a blade

*

i was an orgasm
    i spoke only gibberish
        i was pleasure
            the throb of being alive
                i give thanks to the biscayne boulevard shaman

*

staring at the popcorn ceiling	lying in bed, the day dangles from my windowsill
i linger, the air of a dream	maya angelou's living room
on a small couch watching a film	projected on the wall in front of us
jayne cortez speaks about horoscopes	maya sits in a rocking chair to my right
smiling and swaying,	her legs warmed under a long quilt
i use the bathroom, i see two paintings	one graffiti, stenciled-shapes, flowers
the other a hand drawn image of me	i'm proud to be hanging in her bathroom
i try to take a picture with my phone	when i'm back to the living room
her home is familiar	we did a poetry reading together
once upon a timeless time	maya laughs at the memory we never made
she walks toward the kitchen	prepares us food
homemade biscuits	she hands to me
eat, she says.	never mind how long we've known each other
now is always new	she feeds me

*

sometimes i am a stranger unto myself
freefalling in the eye of what i survived
a kind of flying
really a scar never fades
call it pretty perhaps
dressed as a breeze
approaching unannounced

like a shivering storm
to be a feather for love on a beaming wing
to swim air
everywhere is swimming
sometimes i glow in grief
the gloss of nearly drowning
the mercy of misfortune
she who owns the evening like a supermoon
ballroom dancing on the ocean floor
a periwinkle room with no doors or windows
an eye opening underwater
basement of the world
where living is looking up

*

heaven beneath
weather below under
    ground
if the ocean had eyes
lashes blushing
she who giggles the land
an earthquake tiptoeing
the lover's will
quivering the floorboards of our minds
if walls could talk
    they'd stumble speechless
        and d i s a p p e a r
rooftops sit at our feet
birds worship the ground
whispering about butterflies
moths and cicadas
i'm well-fed on living,
how to rid past lives with a pill
the panic of dream-peeled eyes

a planet of burgeoning trees and smiling breaths

meditating on beautiful gestures

the last impression is always more important than the first

a good-bye baptism

in other words
the water is rising

florida water

i started 2020 jumping seven waves
for yemaya on an ipanema beach

four flowers hand-dipped in prayer
they did not survive the undertow

i was the whole firework show
while my love closed his eyes

impatient with my joy,
a hunger for more than fighting

please, can we be meaningless now
and leave america where it's at?

the whole village in my chest is tired of weeping,
let us organize the heart, community

i'm toothing the picket signs out of my poems as we speak
maybe i'm not a good revolutionary

i am not guided by love,
i want to be it
i want to be drenched
i want to sweat and stink of love
i want to lay and not know where
        the day begins or ends

to be held in my own arms, longer
than a two-week vacation

i want to be a poem that never works,
that does not resonate with anyone.

to be a poem you cannot share
so alive it is so

i sashayed into the new year
iboga heckling my veins

set on being unafraid and triggerless
all revelation and rested shoulders

i caught a fever in bahia
or an ancestor told me, take a seat

write, it is time to write
catch these poems before
you whine about how
we did not answer

this year was a dedication to florida water
the cleansing

little did i know the whole world would be rinsing too. everyone is a running faucet, blood on their hands. can't face ourselves in one another. the vision came to me in egypt and there was nowhere for a lie to hide. i saw god escape religion like a breeze, every sunset a new download, what felt like 50-hour days or a conversation with a metallic scarab that did not make sense until it did. i could see the very beginning and the end. it wasn't so much that it was a big bang, more like a sneeze, the earth shaking us off like a bad cold. so very entitled, convinced our lives are worth something more than now. none of us are too good to suffer. miami taught me the art of killing a mosquito after the bite. the other day i planted a bed of healing herbs. my love brought me two butterflies he found on his walk broken wings hanging from his fingertips, they sat between the rosemary and thyme, incapable of

flying   all flutter and might   to love. fear is a spirit i will not let
in.   cradling a metaphor   the year   is not yet   over

the foreshadowing furlough

florida always reminded me of childhood. either fresh starts or awful endings reminded me of my mother fleeing new york city that one two or third time to port st lucie with the homes that all looked the same in the gated community in the middle of nowhere or that one beautiful home in west palm beach from the '50s with the luscious blooming garden or after my grandfather died and my mom bought a house with the money he left. my white crib, the easy-bake oven, and the big mechanical bird that used to speak to me or the stitched portrait of children flying kites, balloons above my head. there were those summers we visited aunt sabrina and the time uncle shamba came to visit us or when uncle charlie's baby died and i didn't want to leave his arms because he was a man of my making and his eyes sparkled and sang every time he saw me like i was his favorite niece and how i would fall asleep in his earth-toned laugh and trace the lines in his large hands with my tiny fingers. all of the rumors. grown folks talking about him robbing homes. how i'd ride in the middle seat of his cherry-red mustang or how his dimples made more space in a room for the family to relax their shoulders or love one another like for real like love love like they actually found peace in each other's dimples or that time we flew down to miami from new york city to go to uncle orlando's funeral and we stayed in fort lauderdale. i opened the door one morning to see uncle charlie standing there in the doorway and i screamed and cried because it'd been years. he was escorted by the florida state police troopers and i didn't understand at the time the feat my mother had accomplished getting the warden of the prison to release him for his brother's funeral. florida. florida reminds me of open caskets and dress shoes and prisons and beach water where you can see your feet but also that time my mom packed my brother and me in the car in the middle of the night and my stepfather ran after us. she drove off with his hand still in the window and i don't remember if he hit her or not. i just knew love didn't make no sense and it required a lot of back and forth then whispering then looking at each other from across the room with hungry eyes. sometimes love left and never came back and you were lucky if you escaped or if it found you again and this time you could call it by its name and wear it like a new dress on the first day of primary school. florida reminds me of homemade strawberry jello in the fridge and the first nintendo with the duck game and the toy gun and the little dog chasing whatever fell from the sky. i don't remember any ass whoopings or my mother ever raising her voice. this was before the sickness came and she still smiled at me like she wished me up on a star or something like the whole world was still and full and moving slowly and i remember the days at the shore, how she was fun and she would bury me in the sand and i would run for the shells and life was just endless it was endless it was like an endless boardwalk or how years later my brother was flunking out of school hanging with the wrong crowd and she sent him to florida with my aunt like florida was a southern disciplinarian for little black boys from new york city and that one summer i visited and my brother was so mean i learned how puberty turns boys into mean men a rite of passage into patriarchy. florida reminds me of sweaty church sundays with my aunt sabrina and the holy ghost like a janitor of souls or the first time i ever passed out in the middle of praise and worship and i swore god swept through me like i was closer to some divine source than her and my aunt interrogated me the whole ride home what was god like what was god like what was god like what what was it like to have god on your tongue?

highs and lows

his skin was mud leather sweating sun
saltwater ash pacing in drips of smoke
swirling on agitated city corners

a frail waist drowned in wrinkled jeans
a thin hand fidgeting in a front pocket
the cigarette that arms the air

barely lungs, blood breathing
poverty is loving someone more than
you love yourself, scars that refuse to heal

open scabbed men: fathers, brothers, uncles
broken knobs turned loose screws
dreams snuffed from brilliant minds blazed out

melted shoulders bemoaning petty cash robberies
reminiscing redundant afternoons
hunched over vacant lot memories

snorting your mother's gold chain for a quick fix in vein
it's the long lines at the shelter
when they ran out of beds

collect calls at 2am
a toothache in the middle of your head
chewing on the brain bit by bit

fatigue with low-lit vision
a screen on its last percent
a small animal whining

a howl that slaughters the ear
fragile as a punished mouth
portrait of craves

a beggar's palms in the belly
the space between choices and words
calloused hands and calloused hearts

yemaya

i went to see someone about my pain
    and he told me i had to meet the warrior
        at the edge of the sea
            "do not carry anger that is not yours" says el brujo

and just like that
    the sand is a quiet prayer rug
        under folded knee
           deep washed ashore
                rain passing the cheek
          lick salt from lips
      longing for the wide arms of wind
    woozy and restless
rushing toward   the deity of living sea   horse of my heart
      r u n n i n g

to the teacher of tides
    wet whisper of all that swims
        breathing beneath blue watercolor
           here to heal my hurt
            i f a l l

           black mermaid of miracle and pearl
        mistress of moon and star below
      seven glittering waves splash aquamarine
a flamenco skirt   dancing on the sky   lightning fast
      f o o t w o r k

heaven on your shoulders
    arms flirt the clouds
        a migrant bird outstretched
           el brujo rubs my body with the fruit
                and tears the shirt from my back
           mumbling a tongue that teases me faint
      tell me can you hear those thrown overboard
    teetering on the plank

their drowned-out screams sink
        each shriek a shimmering mirror
            i bury my face in the chest of the ocean
                    w e e p i n
            for all the voices remembering me
        god of cerulean scales and gold fins
temper of turbulent rivers roaring rain
        cleanse me of sadness and sorrow
            in the grandest lakes lagoon or stream
                    i offer you papaya
                            coconut and cotton flower
                                deep labyrinth of worlds sunken under
                            lady who levels land
                    tames tsunamis
            queen of atlantis
        dwaraka beneath arabian sea the
spirit of depth
        the mapless mountains inward
            how light goes to rest
            vanishing in the opaque
                    largest body without borders
                        fishing boats filled with dreams that never dock
                            guardian of the glistening ancient graveyard
                                ghosts gossiping without tombs
                        fortune-teller of shivering shells
                soothing these stranger times buzios
        i do not know which ancestor gave me this rage
but i am ready to lay it down
    this bouquet of unbecoming burden
i am ready
        to lay it
                lay it
                        down
                            áshe

the perfect storm

the perfect storm
empties a country of abuelitas
padres hermanos mujeres y niños

a disaster that doesn't seem so natural
waves of wind damaged homes
hovering roofs made of tarp

if you wanted to take land
from a people bent
on resisting colonialism
insert mcdonalds
walmart
or the jones act
or blame it on a storm
of a woman named maria
who grew up in spanish harlem
who reminded us of the western story

as the rich are getting richer
the poor are getting poorer
never mind the wealth that ain't
so common under the foot of US force
the way loss runs through steep hillsides and rivers
swell the veins between vacant towns

we blame the thirsty
but not the corporations that tax water
the shocking doctrines of profit over people
exploited tunes and tones of taino rhythms for tourists and escapism
por la isla de encanta
we, we lament the boriquen tongue in power outages of spanglish
cursing the companies of settler colonial conditions
for the prayers and litanies tears like rosary beads
in the sewers of sorrows where fantasmas sing
from the sore throat blueness of blood

the border between refugee and nomad

migration is the art of fleeing
sad songs for blooming in suitcases
la gente fuerte and worn wondrous
we belong, we belong to each other
before any notion of a nation
no one will understand the tangled trues
of being from here and nowhere
the beaming cocqui that still visits in dreams

they won't write us in history if we don't write ourselves

the uncle who drowned in coronas and ham sandwiches
visions of never playing pro baseball
the aunt who claps the roof of her mouth
when she speaks asthmatic
and always, always, always high
who lost six children to the government
abuela who is always working 2 to 3 jobs
to make up for the guilt of coming to america
and how she couldn't face returning to no running water

and still there are spirits, there are spirits
who know every chupacabra has its day
it is time it is time it is time it is time it is time
for us to take the red fire of our wounds
and weapon our mouths toward new movement songs
remember, *remember* Campos suffering in silence
separated by an ocean, and a language yet still free
free in the love of a people fearless and
always, *always* a hurricane
its always a hurricane
its always a hurricane before the grand exodus
before the grand exodus
the fight for dignity and independence
san ciriaco rattles

rattles rattling in every roar
every roar of revision is history
pa'lante people pa'lante
milagros de movimientos
soar because if we are to live
if we are to live with the fierce force
of knowing anything
anything that is sacred is worth fighting for
bienvenido a la lucha
we are worth
fighting for

choice

i choose the soft corners of your eyes
a wind song swimming blues
of morning and evening beside you
flowered footsteps toward the edge of knowing

i choose a sky in your palms
and snorting an open chest

i choose the child of my letting go
life as we once were made anew

i choose turning the page
watching the ink dry
the pen name of awe and wonder
my hand in yours

i choose the enduring way through
a love that leans and lays lessons
a love that adventures a yes
a love that sees a wall as a window
a cold shoulder as touch
a silence as a garden of breath

i choose us learning alone together
every day is a choice to love ourselves afraid
the way we want and need
we choose one another each life
we return to the bed of our making

i choose the seconds in between
the minutes the hours the days
a love that chooses love

i choose the wet of me
the wet of you
    glisten*ing*

the porch is a throne of small talk

making love in the south is daring
we sizzle and smoke of soil
smudge our homes with groans
the land talks back
drunk on dawn
we live lazily with the song of nightfall
dreaming in the south is sublime

if it would've went how it could've

the fireworks are there to watch us
sprung on droplets of touch
whirling of waves, we leak breath
no one else but us
even when they are
we are enuf for you
it is never too much
or maybe you didn't come
i went to brazil by myself
i fell in love with my grandfather's dimples
chuckling in my cheeks
i catch a dance
swirling above rio on a helicopter
i am my own joy stumbling with grief
i pillow talk with the ocean
scrolling the inner ear of a shell
i am adored and faith-full
i live in the eyes of now
naked with hoodoo desire
we journey beyond perversion
to be wanted even from bunion to crown
dazzling above
was it too much?
the funk of freedom
sweet vines growing around our shoulders
sugar cane, coconut water, and salt
this is how we end by beginning
sharing the picture frame in a living room
a wall of weeping piano keys
a song on a spine
unspeakable rippling
i become a series of movements and tones
you say i love you back and mean it

a state of emergency

twice in a blue moon
in the rhythm section of running
this swamp sway freshwater spring
spiritless spirited home of highway haunts
of conservative billboards blazing
antiquated trails

long arm of land bent
on the map like a waving pistol

we water
keys jingling to the caribbean sea
a field of graves glimmering
on the ocean floor
the sunken guerrero ship soaked
water walking africans
shore shamed

gator grill men
fools for sun squeezed skin
of oranges and juicyfruit
mango juice chins sticky fingers
braided palms in pools of light
tender pebble creeks

we water
whistling in the nodding wind
daffodils rinsed by a breeze
a stream exhales at dusk
cicadas crooning
a diamond back rattlesnake in high grass
flower petals float on the flesh of rivers
agua florida
ponce de leon haunting the fountain of youth
at a genocide theme park
the smudge of the timucua people's slaughter

we
water

fluent in the cursive tongue of hurricanes
tracing the mid atlantic's signature
on our front porches
black seminole high priestess
goddess of the gulf coast
dripping of abandoned dreams
in the lullaby of gnats
the sea as a doorway
of syllables rising
where the land mourns
and the sky chokes
sinking boardwalks
buildings sob of corrupt codes
politicians snorting gunpowder
drunk on stolen votes
trickle-down delusions
panopticon self-surveillance state
a police officer stationed in your bedroom
the judge washed up on our brains
where voodoo priests, santeras, and shamans
pontificate premonitions
and prescribe spiritual baths for mal de ojo

how i-95 cut miami like a fresh wound
seagulls chatter of nonviolent wade-ins
virginia key mangrove snappers
la villa blues bussin through a houseboat radio
drum circles barking in the chest
how these days locals don't visit the beach
avoiding tourist terrorists with neon hats
and sunscreen masks

love bug road trips
dragonflies on a windshield

seven-year war trade
treaties and trials
imported bigotry
pines, palmettos
in florida, the insects complain about the people
we water
bahamian fisherman turtling on key biscayne

when it's race it pours
    four black boys dragged from their names in groveland

    400 bullets grin chewing at the body of a child sleeping under a tree

    a mob the color of burning flesh whitens the streets
    this is the crime no one was charged for

in florida there's no truth
only sentencing in cruel, cruel fragments

saltwater railroad

they don't tell you the water has footprints
or how the ocean has no borders
except which way the tide pulls
still a country to endure
we learn slavery was the living death that began us
a sailing freight train of fugitives
people of the horizon
with hurried hands
the knife of time at a bare throat
the little engine that couldn't
tormented among coral reefs
chasing breath
what did we laugh about?
did our eyes taste of distance?
wailing lashes?
a god-shaped hole in our belly
getaway routes paved in moonshine
walking the plank, hungover
sailing off the horizon's wrist
the hushed indigo of veins
where waiting yawns
where water is seasoned
how salt stings
an open cut running
never looking back
we set sail for red bays
of isolated cays, lowbanks or reef of coral,
rock or grain of sand
or why till this day
it costs an arm and leg to fly
between any caribbean countries
a bloodstream
a railroad of bones
southbound with the fever of freedom

the absurdity of law

illegal to feed the homeless **without** a permit
illegal to sell oranges on the sidewalk
illegal to keep a car you do not use on your property
illegal to skateboard without a **license**
illegal to fall asleep under a hair dryer at the salon
illegal to "**corrupt** the public's morals"
illegal to roll a barrel down the **street**
illegal for a man to wear a strapless dress / gown
illegal to **sing** in public while wearing a bathing suit
illegal to have sex with porcupines
illegal to exchange **gossip**
illegal to **imitate** an animal
illegal to sell your **children**
    Do not fart in public place after 6pm
    Do not shower naked
illegal to have oral sex
illegal to **kiss** your wife's breast
illegal to molest a key deer
illegal to step on a turtle egg
illegal to let go a **helium** balloon
    Do not hang your clothes outside on the clothesline
    Do not molest a trashcan
    Do not have a flower pot without a drainage hole
    Do not lean your bike on a tree in a cemetery
ambling and strolling is a misdemeanor
    Do not bring a pig to the beach
Neon signs are prohibited
    Do not go downtown without at least ten dollars on your person
    Do not get electrocuted for using a self-beautification tool
    while in the bathtub or you will get fined after death
no nudity on stage unless it is a "bona fide" performance
    Do not catch crabs
    Do not wear liquid latex in public
women cannot **expose** their breasts while performing "topless"
lap dances must be given at least six feet away from the patron
only the missionary position is legal
and *of course* they're banning **books**

sign language

a raised fist as a lantern
or an open palm as a line to break
a checkpoint in the sand
or how many chapters in a story
we know a bowed head as surrender
we have all heard eyes sing of the sea
or skin speak the sun
or a belly as a shrine
a mother becomes a mortician
a father becomes a ghost
the wait between planting a seed
and witnessing the bloom
the thorn, an instrument of war

we visit readers to transcribe our loss
we throw shells across a table or floor
to ask questions
felt without flesh
we light seven-day candles on the altar
answers wink at us from another realm
there are ways of reading
without words

the fool

i ran heart-first into the whole sky of it
fragile gift of firsts
if we end unkind and wicked with ways
was it _ _ _ _?
i was not thinking
remembering a mystery, a myth, a map
searching for breadcrumbs of consideration
little clues of compassion
if there is no tribute to the trying times
was it _ _ _ _then? as if apart
are we strangers
were we always
are we a metaphor for something greater
the unraveling riddle
what was that we were?
the whole hum of us buzzing through the days
waking up beside one another
giggles and glares
roaming grocery store aisles
slow dancing with the shopping cart
when we argued about the dishes
the arrangement of furniture
who would throw out the garbage
or which local court jester to vote for
was it _ _ _ _? to be held with regard
traveling the country of our discontent
advocating for everyone else
but us
was it love? Or

is love a commons?

in the fifth year of side by side,
he tells you he's got nothing left
for you
not even tears
no apology will do
after all he is not meant for relationships
just mobilizing them
his heart floods the internet
a tsunami of tears for his people
what a revolutionary man
who cries and shares softness
a stranger staring back at you
through a screen
a timeline of prolific distance
between you and him
what is socialism if it means
his right to be right except
for when it comes to you
what do you call that?
this trope, this boring nightmare
when a man fights for everything but you,
what is the restorative process?
where are the picket signs
the resistance, riots, canvassing perhaps?
a sense of urgency?
who will redistribute this pain?
a heart rationed by rhetoric
splayed into a statistic
a house no longer a home
but an organizing strategy
for every cause but our love
eulogies for strangers
none for your little deaths
what is the name for this triggering?
a quiet town
preserving his reputation   (yours, too)

the indifference to your sadness it seems
what are those scarred years called?
the stink of suffering
in the end
all that matters
is you don't
where is the community for those
who belong to nothing?

wanted child,

did they not teach you where babies come from?
what did you think would happen
you growing inside me
if not another quite possibly
a whole other presence shared
this want to be wanted
your wrath visits the mother of my loving hand
in the parking lot of errands
your frightening fists stomp the steering wheel
the cowardice of it
i cannot unfeel
a daughter i never quite got to be
hold
a cold stare standing beside me at the doctor's office
a forced goodbye, the miscarriage
of our first hello
how did i survive my own screams
too nauseous to reason words
i could not utter in public
i refuse to bring the child you would not choose back
how could you know what you know?
ask of me what you did not have the courage to ask

hand wash only

every time i sit to write about you the phone rings
or the door knocks and suddenly the laundry needs washing
or the grocery list is growing out of the fridge

it nearly has arms, yells demands
the books are piling up and so are the bills
the papers need organizing

or my body fidgets begging to belong again buzzing of want
i cannot listen to songs with lyrics these days
i have turned into what i remember most about my father as a little girl

liquored lips, all i listen to is jazz
sometimes it's smooth other times it's messy
or whatever genre there is for missing what could've been

a service that streams, a river of thoughts i sit by
and worship what channels through
when i look at you now i see all i could not see before

i see myself more clearly
sometimes i am in the kitchen
and i catch a memory floating in the dishwater

leftovers clog and settle in the drain
i slip my fingers through the soapy image
and watch colors change

it's empty now and there's grease all over the sink
tears ache down the cheek into a bowl or on a fork
why can't i just wash the dishes without you

what i miss most was the way my eyes
kissing your face was delicious
a meal i savored secretly

devouring your dimples for last
or us laying on the couch,
my head stitched to your heart

my favorite dreams were the ones i had in your arms

it is the things i don't want to remember
that trip me up on my way to the bedroom
your fist to the broken ironing board

delirious with anger
your bandaged knuckles, a bloody lie
we laughed away with the dinner party

i shouldn't have gone and gotten myself pregnant
i didn't know you were pretending
to mean what you meant

i was just trying to wash your clothes that day
so when you got home it was soft
soft as our smiles the day we met

how was i supposed to know your shirt would shrink

frank, ocean

we'll never be these kids again
the start of something—
deep down, always wanting
we float in a rental car
on a highway of borrowed time
the radio hisses a playlist of past lives
a hamlet in upstate new york
birthday suits in a forest
bare feet along a cold stream
i am a mermaid on a rivering road
we make time
we create seconds, minutes, hours—days
we fuck like forever,
forget the trees towering over us
a trance of crickets
eavesdropping on promises
lost and found along the way
you are my corner of the earth
we hide and seek the crevices
cartwheels on the front lawn of life
we shower with stars
and count until we are winded
blanketed beneath one another
a sea of moss

sanibel will always be ours

these are different shades of blue
flesh thoughts, swelling desire
our appetite for waves
your face shimmering
in the great garden of baths
i follow this feeling wherever it moves
the bloom of tides
a playground for moans
the wishes of waves
nibbling ears
mushroom clouds sigh
a ribbon in the sky
i follow your kiss
we weather
a sermon of salt
a body as a boat
wiggling out of our shells
i press my ear to your chest
we shriek with laughter
and toss our skin
lovers of this lighthouse island
wet with escape

castaway

i did not want to write a poem full of corpses
so i wrote a sacred pink blue sky jeweled on the horizon
laughter as the loudest star sleeps
humor hugs every ache whole
how heavy heads lay after a long day in the humid heat
caribbean moon sighs and joyous dreams

i did not wish to speak
of what should not be spoken
so silence breathed into all
the words, a haunting. i come from
a language that does not write itself, our ancestors speak
hurricane, a thunder tongue shivering tides
and a petty revenge, the mid atlantic is a vexed aunty
rattling rivers and roofs, ready for reckoning
knocking at the chest of men

on the other side of now
there is a door where we return
every island is a hip swaying
between here and there
a float in the dance
to belong
rocking in the arms of the edge
where the sea is an emerald flag
and palm trees praise the air
every shore is an altar
of remembrance
embraced on purpose
pickney of the sun ray

where prayer trembles
the light or how a storm retreats
we marvel and move eternal,
unforeigned and unlost
hips hollering, elbows flapping like fanning flames

bare feet chant in the sand or in a concrete jungle
love taps quake the nape of the earth's neck
where daughters of diaspora dream
and inherit journeys of flesh
where a smile is also a scar

or how my grandfather came to see about us
years after he died
wearing my uncle's face
dimpled and shining eyes
like two wet black beans
baptized by a spirit
rum slapped on his breath
charming man and all he was
checkin' on his grandbabies

fear not death
we visit kinfolk there, lingering
in the blood, where the ocean hums
tribe of the great abyss
a not knowing from where or what we come
and still to arrive before they could conquer

us, we came by shipwreck, by wind and wave
pushed into the water
splashing and shaking
the wound teaches us to remember
where tomorrow glows
listen to the animal clawing within
a rooster caws directions between this world and the next
there are roads that cannot be mapped
and there are streets that do not have names
we ran away into the okra-tinted mountains
seeking maroon hills
i was born borderless, mounting a dollar van
like an orisha scribbling visions
on a train or in an airport

traveling ritual voice and time
i was born of distance
in between now and then

maroonage

surrender is not in our blood
drumskins beside a bonfire
flames flickering in fruitland park
in the snickering swamp of runaways
we rehearse freedom
give us liberty or death
we stew a world our babies marvel at

prayer is a place of no blame
we who fled toward a southern star
in the depths of darkness we lit up
with our ancestor's visions in our eyes
the battle of okeechobee
of bonds and bail
sabana systems
despachos en formade su libertade
fort mose on the edge of a salt marsh

dear dream defenders
remember the field of flowering
palm thatch houses
a people of steps stones banners and bellows
we are the raft of feverish fortunes
principled as portraits
i meditate on our forever now

the great grievances we woke with
waiting and witnessing
wanting something more for each other
even when we did not
know how to say the sorry of our seeking
in a local bar together around a pool table
the ravishes of our hungering
the next day and thereafter
we showed up and out
grip the boulevards

scheduled days of dinners
playdates with our hereafter we could not keep

when i look back i know we were closer than we are
walking with the shifts of our changing same
the commissioner meetings and happy hour conversations
hood week volunteers hoping to make the homeless more than smile
shame is a way to motivate perhaps
we question purpose and answer the call
purple nights and blush sunsets
bailing out our expectations
racing and ranting through the intricacies
the way we want for others as ourselves

this is how we lived with the pressure to make change now
and if we didn't do what we said we'd do
we worried for fear of not being who we said we'd be
each of us aspiring to live up to the holy how of our name

can we *actually* dream together?
in the glades of our evering

smoke signals

a little haiti altar of grassroots meetings
backyard of radical imaginings
praise the corridors we conjured
each room a curation of gifts
vendors of visions and versions
songs sit on the shelves

art basel is a colonial project
where the rich wash money
through over-priced paintings
and displace residents
with tourists ditzyisms
unaffordable instagram feeds

we decolonize our creativity
painters poets musicians
the great eviction show
a theater of our dimensions
capitalism on display
we ride a moving truck through wynwood
the belongings of a home
sobbing on a side walk

the urge to awaken our cares
a ritual for demonstrating our values

an art to surviving loss
the smoke of being alive

angels waging sit-ins on a canvas

for purvis young

pregnant paintings
swollen with boat people stuttering on yellow sunsets
scribbles of marching
a wall of disrespect,
the rubells gentrify a legacy
scraps of tired wood and fractured doors
found objects nailed all
over town, shotgun shacks
syncopated brushstrokes sail a southern embrace
bare knuckle dreams
vietnam war veterans, refugees
slaves of a color palette
ghostly figures moving, a showdown of buildings
shivering black squiggles strutting bodies
praying or grieving masks
big-headed brilliance, the struggle to accept
a mirror or window, the improvisation of hands
channeling history in a fire hazard world
meditating on morsels of miami
slumlords and syringes
the madness of never knowing
your gifts as gifts
methods of survival.

magician city

now for their last and final magic trick
developers disappear a neighborhood

now you see it
now you don't

solidarity

beside you
we sit unsaid
your smile, my face
your hurt, my hands
your laughter, my dimples
your tears fall from my eyes
your tired arms hang from my heavy shoulders
your feet in my shoes
this breath is ours
this life
ours
care by care
we carry on

for freedoms

after our basel

somewhere an artist pulls at the seams of themselves
writing until their fingers bleed
until the paint runs dry and the canvas crawls
and the country is a museum of movement murals

somewhere an artist is soaking their toes in ballet slippers
walking on tight ropes
rehearsing themselves hungry
a recital for every picket sign raised
somewhere an artist is gluing bottle caps
to the soles of their shoes
tapping at the times
stomping down tyranny
turning a street corner into a stage
rapping the evening news

somewhere an artist battles their breath
mumbling lyrics
counting syllables on their fingers
for the abolition of sixteen bars

somewhere an artist is pitching a portrait,
throwing bullet points at a meeting of minds
for the movies that lace us with revolutionary vision

somewhere an artist bares arms, sculpting a fist in plaster,
wheatpasting a window on wall
wrestling the sky
scraping at developers trying to erase a neighborhood

somewhere an artist tires their lungs raw
conjuring the wind for a song that heals our hurt into homes
planting flowers in weapons and beating drums with dreams

this is for the citizens wading through the process
the father mopping our hallways,
the mother riding three buses and two trains
to drop her daughter to school,
raising our children,
nursing our elders,
making our beds,
for the migrant families
summoning the sun to set and the fields to fly,
picking our fruit and laying the ground for our cities
they are all artists, creating and shaping our country
clenching courage like a truth telling poem or photograph

for the artist who dares to love, to risk and rally
meeting in houses, churches, and storefronts turned studios
laying the blueprint for freedom
gathering a people toward purpose
for the will to change
for the freedoms we cherish
and the stories yet to be told

art is a way through
a vote and a choice
how we shape and shift the culture
how we get free

for the kids who live

after parkland, florida

what becomes of children who survive us?

indigo rosebuds or sunflowers risen of landfills
voices made of tire swings and milk crates
stick figures in sand drawn by fallen twigs
who looks history in the eye, grins
imagines worlds away within
the power to better
love above law
risk above comfort
for the lost and departed
wandering in memories unspoken

who will unruin this generation
their right to bloom brilliant,
stumble or fall
enchanted by tomorrows

here's to the kids who live in liberty city
bounce house and jumping rope
where no bullet lives to tell a fairytale

for the kids whose toes dip on shores
songs made of sandcastles and broken glass
rinsed by rushing water
return home to a land that welcomes another way
where no child is a refugee

here's to the kids who live to see a world without walls
to the kids who cross-
examine borders, time zones, and language
who dab presidents out of rooms
and judges out of courthouses
a vote with values

music with no commercials

for the preservation of rivers, parks, and birds
to the kids who live
praise wind, light, and rain

here's to the words they speak
trembling of blameless rage
old spirits thundering on tongues

here's to holding hands with fortune-tellers
to the kids who read palms
a gift with no return address
a world without begging fingers
to the kids who live in food-desert boroughs
jubilant with full bellies and crops of care
thirst quenched from free fountains

here's to the kids who live in tears turned from laughter
to serious play
may they never know caskets
before grayed hair and wrinkled skin
like crinkled poems in a old lover's hold

here's to the ones who live in photo albums
images teased of dreams
bless the child who remembers
who questions
and answers with courage
or the kids who live to bury their elders
bare a new story made possible
a test, a struggle, a journey that reveals the heart

here's to the kids who live
who live and dare us
stand aside
may they embarrass us

show us who we are

here's to the kids who live in us and never leave
resting in the dimples of a mirror
stretching through a glance
how many kids must die for us to live?

here's to the kids who live in us
to the kids who live and demand
we act
in the doing
here and now
awestruck and unafraid

garner

for erica

before we name it
when they came for her love
she yelled
when they came for her child
she fought
when they came for her

                                she could barely get out of bed

tooth and nail

                                she braved

folklore and flesh
balled fist and prayer hands

                                what dreams keep us up

thick   in mourning
chest pain
aching shoulder
lower back
or tired feet

                  our body keeps score

well-wishes do nothing
grief
don't   open blinds
                 pay bills
                 feed mouths

                                being woke won't bring back the dead

it is day to day
heavy
swollen breath
brow of sweat
the whole world could march
it would never fill missing shoes
each word dispels

                    making sense of loss
                    we owe her   to herself
she who cries out
memories scatter us
                                        a heart is a map of courage
a heart is an electromagnetic field

        a familiar drum   voice   story
of pulse
                                a portrait of gravitational pull
a heart gathers tribe
in the doldrums of days
                                when the world is a blue funk
wreckage
                    bluer than blue blood
she is a truth telling shore
assembles the people
weep   cleanse   tend
your heart
                    is a frontline

trace a wound
cradle listening
hands
        mind
                how we butterfly in battle
eternal as reckoning
quiet strength
disarm a lie
mourn   reconcile   be made whole
                                        there is doing
                                        then there is undoing

                    love is
                    what love
                    does
                                undo

tell me
how far we've come
and yet so far
       to go.

in justice

after audre lorde

howling in the wound of words,
a tongue trembles with the tension of truth
the difference between poetry and rhetoric
is there's a world outside your door
knocking inward, a voice hungers fearless
wooed by courage
a deliberate impulse
the ability to turn a knob
alter or shift
action
a window is a mirror
of risk, a poet writes
to balance the scales of power
yet feels the absence of power
perhaps instead of rape
i ought to say he forced a sweating throb
liquored moans mangled morning a roofie stone
turned me inside out studded wet worn
too tight busted bruise came and went
i was a ghost a rage no one can see
i killed myself a little to enter
the memory so close
i choose not to resurrect the devil in details
and the country still a culture of take or be taken
violently the united states is a forced entry
on stolen land the supreme court weaponizes words
against flesh law is made

still a poem is not a knife or gun
or food
unless the knife or gun is a pen
or clothes
a pen is only a sword
of feelings

not a home
not louder than a bomb
is not flesh or blood
not a condom or pill
cannot unrape you
nor undo your doing
yet a poem is a doing still
warbling within
an ear eye mouth or touch
a living beneath words
how we respond to power
reveals our power
more or less
a flex or relinquish
tug, push pull demand or plead
a wrist dancing between fist and open palm
to kill or be sacrificed
murder is murder
i aborted the child
it did not leave me like a dove or bittersweet farewell
i sucked the life i did not want away
the proof is in the pudding i cannot swallow

a poet writes to balance the scales
any child that dies
cannot undie in a poem
nor can a jury undie our children
there are no words to heal or bring back the dead
remember
you cannot unkill a part of yourself
with dreams or kisses
poetry or rhetoric
awards accolades pensions
money or comfort
marches or protests
judges or prisons
losing a child is a suicide

the whole world silent
a voice lost in the difference
between killing yourself and killing yourself
what we resist will amend
or slaughter us
there will be others
there were others

what say audre lorde to margaret garner of power?
the difference between poetry or rhetoric
is a choice between lesser evils
whether killing your children is killing yourself
whether you kill yourself or your children
a final word singing from a grave

shifted by the missing
maddened by the hold
power is in the wave that moves
the way change is god
so is spirit

soul sees through
or like love
the more you control
the more it controls you
the difference between poetry and rhetoric
is dareen tatour

because a poem is not a knife or gun or bomb
yet a poem can so enrage a nation to imprison a poet
who attempts to balance the scales
agitates
a people power
to do
change
when a foot
is on your neck

it does not matter
how you get it off

what words you say
what weapons you use
knife or pen
so long as you do
is survival

and it becomes less and less
important what someone thinks about
how you resist
unless of course
they are willing to take the foot off your neck too

her

for women's march global

she who un-ruins us
who fears her own tongue

loosened words direct as kisses
sung of partition heart or body part

trafficked in the distance
born of a mouth on the run

she who risks riots and braves
eyes on a frontline

who heals earthquakes and conjures tsunamis
through despair or neglect

force of nature.
she who plants rubies that sunset tills

a breeze carries gold
light across leaves

she who presses the earth to replenish itself
between furrows of terror or torment

who defended us from mobs and militias
she who befriends trees that bare no fruit

who sweeps dust mid-day off root and readies rain
rids rooms of looming words

saves misfortunes thrown out on running streams
waves of daughters left in canoes washed ashore

she who shades under a date palm
her mother's laughter in the background
anywhere she smiles is a revival

a woman survives silence or memory
dismissive regimes dictators or death

she who mourns to remember
what the governed rather forget
we are who raises us

a story

every child is an old ending
a new list of demands
broken taboos and treaties

she who chose hijab over veiled spirit
crazyhorse over oil canteen

who sifts soil and teargas canisters for flowers
she who surrenders with honor

a woman's sword sharpened by wind's teeth
her voice never dies

ancestors' candor
kidnapped by a commercial for lipstick

she who bloodied diamonds
who wept thighs and scorched laws

her fist a wrath of fingers loving each other
a strength in numbers.

she, who lives in a remote village
who beheads her rapist at night
    on a busy street corner

and spits up a scarred
moon

it is worthy to give god praise

for oluwatoyin salau

did i tell you they murdered
my sister who was myself?

this rerun of the worst episode
in american history   tiptoeing

again   i am fighting for someone
who does not love me back

for true   as the word say
does not   love they self   or us

numb drunk ego
black as my brother he will not fight for me too

until i'm a hashtag or caught on camera not talkin' back
black like a sit-in or a coffin

shimmering in the grave of a meme
black like

a punch line
laughing at my busted lip

everywhere i look
i am coarse   curl colored

head wrapped   heavy with hurt
healing harmonica dreaming of breath

called a kiss some places
is also a hug   some say

what is a movement
that cannot hold   us tender

what is a man that is not a man
but a wound of weapon

broken   and   breaking
everyone near capable of loving more

than themselves
if not sorry always sorry

unwilling to undo
the work it takes to be luminous

infinite star gazing
lest we pay in sex or pleasure porn

my death so sexy
i'm worth less alive

we will not survive   this madness
this denial   this mirror   that does not know its own face

lovelessness cannot make a heart whole
we stay one two maybe three restorative circles

away from all the backlogged rape kits gathering dust
in the dirty draws of our lovers

all the little girls in my voice gone missing
meet in my poems thrifting the blues

unsilenced and worthy of mention
the revolution will be a resurrection

of roads unpaved with good intentions

      a tired waistline
a shower
      a safe bed
a nightmare nesting
      my obituary

the ceremony put to rest
who will survive   what survives   us

maroon poetry festival

We even survived the intrusion of the police
twice they came, but poems kept up,
kept hushed, in candlelight n whispers.
The words got out!
     —ntozake shange

emory douglas sitting in an arm chair
talking about revolutionary art

the last poets in our kitchen

sonia sanchez on the couch
reminiscing the time the panthers
showed up to her front door

as much as things change
some stay the same

we gather:
the barber,
the doctor,
the teacher
hand-crafted children
running through a playground
of our organizing
a feast for freeing

ntozake sitting in a rocking chair
beneath our mango tree
in the backyard
with a cocktail in her hand
smoking a newport

a large industrial fan plugged into the dj booth outlet
june's wet breath in our little haiti backyard

the sweet muck of her smile
the police wear jealous eyes
we hurried her into the house
"ohhh i wish i would've worn my blue hair!"
ntozake screams with excitement
waiting on danny and phil to negotiate the night
the officers of buzzkill out front
we sat mischievous as midnight
giddy with raucous poems

it is nearly a year later,
she died in her sleep

i am in my beauticians chair
blueberry curls,
dye dripping along my forehead

    her smile
    her smile
    her smile
in my face
a citation for which there is no summons

i am celebrating a woman i love who loved me before

for sonia

There is no place

for a soft/ black/ woman

   —sonia sanchez, from "Present"

                              like

i mean

                         who's gonna take

the words

                         Blk/ is /beautiful

and make more of it

than Blk/capitalism....

Who's gonna give our young

blk/ people new heroes

   —sonia sanchez, from "blk / rhetoric"

it is easier to imagine the end of the world than to imagine the end of capitalism

   —fredric jameson, from "Future City"

as if we did not lose another
as if life were never so convenient and guns so easy to reach
our country so trigger happy these days
or sad depending on who's dying today

      depending on the touch

the moon raises my rivers yesterday i leaked all around the house
a bad cough and a cloud lookin' over my shoulder as i wrote
and though i cry

i am celebrating a woman i love
who loved me before i knew myself to be

what blooms in the blood
what scratches the voice
trembles words

every day is a new mourning
another fight, we live
to dance between tears
beating on
our faces

i am tired of strength

when i first showed up to the community organizing meeting
i uttered the word poetry
and their faces sunk with confusion

who's got time for poems when the worlds on fire?

    and your brother's body on your front door
    and your sister's been missing for weeks.
    and your dad got laid off and your mother gone mad with mothering
    and your uncle locked up and your aunt need a fix i mean life can get ya down
    and out

but when the organizers were weary
    and all the marching wore them down
    and all the meetings ending in arguments
    and all the foundations brought out the snakes
    and all the trauma piled up on their desks
    and all the campaigns ended with politicians

    i offered poems in their palms like petunias
    revolutionary and blushing shades of plum

i fed them sonia sanchez
and jayne cortez
and june jordan
and pat parker
and carolyn rodgers
and every poem still pierces true
like yesterday's battlefield is tomorrow's front yard
still all my heroes fighting depression
some lived to see what they fought to prevent

and we ought to keep our hopes high but all this comfort
and security got our institutions kidnapped in broad daylight
treaty torn and tricked bamboozled by the beaming brilliance of greed
got our babies programmed for numbness   content is

        and what is an enemy if we do not know who our friends are?

            and who is a comrade these days?

when the poems are good depending on who repost them
depending on who fetchin' for awards

    and who will feed our activists our organizers freedom if not the poets?

we are losing our frontline warriors to suicide
        and is not choosing to fight a sort of sacrifice, a kind of offering?

    all our children have become altars to the liberation front

    the other day we lost amber evans
    baby girl found in the scioto river, she was 28

    and before that it was erica garner,
    a heart full of storm and lightning, she was 27

    and before that it was marshawn mccarrel
    on the steps of the ohio state house
    hunted by the haunting, he was 23

bassem masri our palestinian brother from another mother
what about ferguson
what about edward crawford
what about darren seals
what about

how our dreams smell of tear gas and milk
we cry trumpets
and turn tables
in the corners of our hopes we rhythm and blues

and though i cry
i am celebrating a woman i love

she who turned the pen in her hand to a grenade
haiku homegirls
folklore florist flung stories into our minds planted
orchids and daffodils sunflowers

she who shivered the sky rain showers and sun sets born of her blessing
the flesh of her words
kindred sistuh who wrote for daughters of movement
who say do and act
the call, response resist riot of our rebellious laughter
as we readied our reasons for writing we armed ourselves
with her poems
a strategy for organizing the heart
prophetic prayers
a smile made of spirituals and birth pains

these days it hurts to write
every sentence is a false promise
                              is we or is we not tryin' to get free?
and when the poems do what they do they get it done.

sistuh sanchez
    eternal fellow firespitter

baaaad to the bone
i never met a poet who loved us like you do.
all of us.

and when my anger knocks the wind out my weeping
i sit on the hills of your humming words and feast
of all the ways we got to get to where we are going
in the quiet mirror of a poem how to be human

shake loose
arms outstretched summoning us
uncool and truth telling care

how to heal in the cathedrals of hands
this is a poem for you and for us
for all the poems that sistered us in this ancestral war

all the lines somersaulting

sistuh, you are our north star
in our darkest nights

drizzling moonshine

for ntozake shange

there is the making of magic moods memories meanings made of sweat and
blood tears and how we save ourselves with laughter sister say we haven't lost
nothin but an apparition you were the wind we day dreamed in praying a word
would hold us in the hovering hem that dresses all our skies real recognize real
sometimes i am the loose screw too and i done talked away all the breaths left in
me you storm you rally you river and reason us who can't call it lest our intuition
blows us in the direction when our slurred whiskey ways bring spirits in realms
of tomorrows how our pleasure is a place that cannot be touched, sister you car-
ried us and created us in the image of drizzling moonshine shooting stars in awe
filled eyes you iglesia de la gente whose souls could not be rented nor sold lines
like strands of hair braided in a kitchen mouthfuls of generations sippin on bru-
ja brew you who bellied and boxed god. became her. every daughter comforted
in the rocking chair voice of mothering songs on a front porch come sundown
sister who wrote too for the fire escape women birds tipping their hats to her
feet all our hysterical hearts freed thru smiling scars and scabs we live forever in
your palms read by other magic making ladies i am broken beside myself with
where the world wonders on without your elder visions in these days so tuff we
honor you sister ancestor now a raging love in all our veins as we inhale new
days we could not see without you. Tatted on our spirit tortured tongues, rose
water lenses waging cleansing wars for our weary conversations with fists and
fights for the hooded and baggy panty poet tending to the nudges and loneliness
of pussy portals moanin' thru stretches and reaches of wet journey sex Sister
architect of contradicting translations thot fantasies conjurin in the swells of
highways when they told me my voice was too sage strong, that i shouldn't
speak out of turn, that i was too beautiful to be the blues when all i wanted to
do was weep with wounds for all the ways i discovered the women within the
nonverbal songs we hum sippin on tea midsummer growin pains you was there.
when all we wanted was a slow dance chest to chest listening. ntozake the first
miracle poet i read with a sassy lady spirit so ancient tru real tlk and relevant
now timeless. there was a familiar whisper made the flowers bloom her name
and she spoke the word on our streets. praise be her awe of language of women
who loved thru nightmares and fck bois gals overcomin insecurities blk grl
magic queen silent spells naming us all our glory in goddess slang. i'm searchin
the words for all the lives we share between them. Grateful for who she was

and who she wasn't. i'm just grateful. so grateful she was here. we shared this earth this breath this life. may she rest. may she finally rest in peace. and turn the heavens into a disco house party with all our greats watchin' ovr us. may we make them proud

daughters of the doorway

to move for love is to miss yourself

for who you was before you is to be

she who arrives in the aftermath of a storm

who warbles with realms of reasons for being here

laboring for the hoodoo homes of our black magic families

the royal embrace of flaw and force

healing herselves sweet tea swinging hips

a waist that whistles of eleke beads,

sequins skinned sistering visions

rhythms spin rippling rituals

bathwater worship worthy

we barefoot butterflies favored by spirits

dawn double-dutching on our shoulders

dazzling crown of locs

a chorus of curls

finger coils waving at the wind

snatched edges brilliance braided biblically

beneath our scalps miracles on heavy rotation

a goddess dressed in a gown of courage

basking in ancestral attitude

a garden made of carefully crafted hands

planted in a lover's sky, planets marvel

at the bronzed blueprint of our beauty

the future twinkling in our eyes

giggles of gold

we glow gracefully sculpted by sunlight strutting in our blood

here's a portrait for the portal

daughters devoted to the deity of a doorway

where dreams come and go

hanging on the hinges of our tender headed hearts

sitting on the ledge of a window

in our mother's womb we write

waiting on a world to die.

a poem for agnes furey

for years i hurt everyone that i loved.

and i measured love by how much pain

someone would take from me.

   —Leonard Scovens

on the other side of grief
we forgive
from the ashes of hurt
never forget
we forgive
eye for eye
we see what we want to
though we may not know how
we knew we would
forgive
the gift of giving
ourselves

every media minute

america's hysterical hands drip blood
    a pointing finger uninward
the people scroll over bodies
    wet dreams of war
we want to believe we aren't dying too
    and the joy is sad.
    and the art is sadder.
when will we live, we think in words.
    and i am a sound.
they tell me love is hard
work but why does it come
so easy?   i haven't clocked in
    i don't want this love to tire
or go on strike for better wages
    or lose itself in a bottle
    at a lonely bar
i am tired of protest
    everything here is a job
    even love
and that is how i know
they have trained us to become
what we loathe
    to desire what disguises us
    to be the executed and the executioner.
i had a friend who had a friend
    and they are no more.
he was so busy being himself
    he couldn't try just being
    for a change.
maybe if we market love like a selfie
or
maybe offer a stimulus package for feelings
    we don't allow ourselves to feel
maybe then we can communicate
    or at the very least
we can laugh at the hypocrisy

of our silly predicament
insanity is the father of invention
    he's a rolling stone.
the christians are clinging to their god
    more than ever before
rickety religions reveal rickety men

    been there
    done that

i want a god no american can worship
i want a god who doesn't want to be worshiped
    who isn't insecure
    or condescending

i want a god who doesn't put borders
    around heaven
i want a god who smuggles souls
    pass patrol officers
    sins seated in the trunk
    of his four-door chest
    thundering down walls

      i want a god
      don't you?

we need something
something greater than ourselves
there's a whole lot of religion
and not enough god
to the god that shivers the leaves
kisses the rivers
brings you to your needs

      i want a god
      don't you?
something greater lives within ourselves

i want a god who returns
    prayers to sender

        i want a god
        don't you?

we need a god
who laughs with/at us
a god who loves

national immigrant integration conference

huddled in homes
    beneath hovering helicopters

blood blazing across the bodied boulevards in brazil
    a scream licks the eye

out of this war with wants
    we wobble in and out of words

tender rhythms looting the heart
    sheikh jarrah drenched in skunk water

swelling streets of suitcases
    palestinians kneel in a prayer

the mosque is a dust cloud
    rubber-coated bullets

                    who burns a mosque during ramadan?
the pulse of a wrist demonstrating
    poverty is man-made

battling mounting police presence in colombia
    earthquakes do not know

how to pronounce the word *border*
    breaking buildings and manmade laws

haitians hanging on history
    a homeland of make-believe debt

the residue of revolution
    hope for security, for protection

temporary as today
    you cannot deport disaster

unnatural as sea levels rise
    the forest in a fire

a poem is a portal hissing of visions
    protests sweating the brow

wages worn on a wrinkled woman's face
    waiting at a bus stop

balancing her loves in wearied hands
    a heavy bag weighing on her shoulders

how to feed a country
    kidnapped from the candle in her lover's eyes

looking forward to yesterday
    on the front porch of the lower end

restless as election night
    or low-income housing

somewhere else
    a field day with our skin
    long as today ago
    a sky in the head
    hand-me-down healing
    a little bird told me
    temperance

may all your cups be filled
    burn your uniforms
    unionize your hearts
    the soil breathes
    begging for seed, sun, and water

a wave the length of love

the devil you know

taxes the air we breathe
privatizes the water
profits off homelessness
strangles the land
injects hormones in animals
rapes the people and rewards the rich
charges you for being sick
sends a bill to your loved ones with interest when you die
laughs at us coughing up our lungs
gulping water lead dripping off our chins
buys private ships to the moon
dances with your demons

the selfish individualistic part of you
the one who rather not have a foot on your neck
or who shows up to the rally after sipping sweet comfort
at a corporate gig that pays you just enough to die   a little slower
and tithe to the community foster care

how being black or women or queer or trans or other
or human or in humane computer or code able bodied
or ten fingers ten toes running or right or wrong

how none of it matters
when the earth is a handwritten letter from the past
a ghost sculpted in blood
cities sweating bitter memories
flooded by crawling maggots and swollen hurt
how the sewers sing of old sidewalks
and cool breezes are of fairy tales
we spoon feed our children in the heat
and we were never ourselves had we known who we are without
greed a world decorated by betrayal

if we had a sense of humor we'd be more radical
more migrant than citizen

we'd breathe the air clean and ration our resources
gathering hugs and holds set to bloom
in pebbles of rain reasoning with riverbeds
rinsing in daylight
ridding pipelines and fossil fuels
we'd melt all the guns
choose the scar
the moist in the back of our knees
the lick between knuckles
mocking evil and all its ill designed destruction
bulldoze the walls and plant windows
where widows weep beautiful green lakes
hushed in our cradling arms
we'd become the tiny brooklet
kissing creeks
we are near a point of no return
a wounded woman scorned temper sharp
as a thousand shards aimed at one direction

i am weary for weeping
me too she whispers, me too.
the earth said.

the most important election is in the heart
the campaign of soul
a candidate measured by their courage
in the midst of
the enduring strength of love
voting for the inner standing
how we make a way through no way
in a basement church
or a high school auditorium
a family living room

these days
insanity is the sanity
stifled sobs   despair distress   thrill

praise the people's power the poet laureates of the poor
careworn anthems soaring from the keyholes of closed-shut doors
the whistle of who and why
the architect of self-determination

if you gon vote
vote with your spine
a head held high
vote with the way you love
a gut singing soft cities sleep dreaming of protests
the ballot is not a bullet but it can be a border or a bridge
    you choose
how you gon vote

pour into
each other
how mourn those we've lost
how help hold the grief
vote with childcare

how you nurse the sick
lending someone your car
pay fair wages
vote by listening to the land
resist The artificial division of our deaths
held together by a common thread of concern

self-determined
reliance
respect
the body is a ballroom of grief and despair

    we the life
    we the chosen
    we the freed
    migrant rebel lovers

we the word workers
we the shoeless and standing tall
we the houseless and housing hearts
we the teachers still students
we the farmers in the field
we the shamans being healed

revolution
is not spectator sport
silence is a noise too

somewhere there is an incorruptible spirit
re-remembering a time when we voted with the thoughts in our mind
it begins with you loving you enuf to love me
as i am you
we are the country's consciousness rising
we are only as powerful as our vote made in the flesh
a voice bravely raising up the reverberating new visions

a livable love

for ruth wilson gilmore

where possible is a presence
let the hummingbird of hardworking hands
an uprisen dream in the shape of now
let the people be deliberate and honest
as a farmer's crop or a child's laughter
door-to-door tenderness

sister,
surely you were a vision, a prayer, a promise
a voice in the head of all our hearts
unmade by remembering
where forgiveness is a collaboration

freedom is here, a song falling
from the dented cheeks of our imaginations
we dance in your dimples
where difference is a commitment to beauty and truth
are we tomorrow yet?

tell us

where life is precious
life is precious
to reach across our questions
the abolition of doubt
something is happening
in the darkest room of our minds
a light switch
a knowing
a testimony from the margins
a livable love

realms whistling of possibilities
where bars become a breeze

and borders become bridges
the imagination as a playground
a monument for stories
grassroots grown from soil

where the land is free
when the food don't do
what our hunger needs
what nurtures and fuels
the void to be and exist
nothing is impossible
or out of reach

we give thanks
for the liberators of language
cartographer of conjured realities
we shatter to shift the shape
and widen the horizon of our listening
let the unforeseeable
transform and transmute the harm
an ode to the people
healing is our inheritance

lotus flower

i was born eternal on the dancing tongue of a flame
drizzled in mountain air we fortified our spirit in the fire
folklore foot drums mystical labor pains
soul crickets candlelit in the foreground
a griot guardian of the crossroads

with the blessing of music we paid homage to the dead
and burn the devils in the dust of ourselves
truth illuminated the people
smoke swirled signals reveal who we fear in our facing
ritual rinses hurt rattling revolution
kindled in the darkling, hushed

we've always known passions other than warfare
gathered tribe in the smell of a storm singing
baptized maroon mouths smoldering
glowing ancestors whistling
a sun setting within
where the town sleeps like a wing
and dreams are altars shining shrines
i listened to the earth talk
and rage became reason
the dance between heal and harm

love is the choreography of catastrophic tenderness
the journey between lightening touch and evening star

give yourself back to you

be kinder to your you
my me earth-raised love-toned
uncountried wind
medicine bath of hands
a drop of sweet honey sun,
a tinge of rum-drunk moon
offer your eyes
become patience
follow the map of your voice
unselfing search
the guidance of your gifts
the swift turn of hips
a refusal to break
the arrival
you are the very love
of your living
the ritual of reach
watercolors of a wet waist
trembling soil
thrifting stars of you
a leaking heart
runneth over
everness
gather among those who twirl
oracle of praying feet
touch the land
betray the syllables of silence
the scandal of truths
scraps of poems shedding secrets
enormous as suffering
measure a moment by its uncertainty
standing still in eyelids
the speed of a tear

i am

i am a flowerpot sitting on the subway platform
dreaming of a southern sky
i am the southern sky
bruised hues of blues
an inner city with an ocean front view
a holy ghost tongue possessed btwn the pews
sleepless in the twilight
a vision board invisible to eyesight
loose hips humming under summer porch lights

i am the djembe drum rhythms spun
between love-drunk knees
i'm a runaway river
a sawed off shot gun creeping through the leaves
a kiss that quivers
a machete that bleeds

i am the bananas on josephine's skirt
a brown liquor flirt
the gardenia in billie holidays hair
i'm a blues song in a cigarette's glare
a beaded zulu hat on makeba's head
bob marley's lock a natty dread

i am marcus garvey's last microphone
ancient lady of grace nefertiti's royal thrown

i am a poem handwritten by la lupe on the malecon
i'm a grassroots meeting of orishas
in the basement of a brownstone
a homegirl homegrown and magic
a mermaid of memory swimming thru tragic times

i am the one that got away
i am the love i never had
a cypher of butterfly wings

i'm a little girl who had big dreams
and prayers in my mother's purse

i am the color of saturday
bouncing off the walls
i drizzle in the wind like a sun shower's shawl

i am the final hour
before the moon rests
i'm what a day looks like honest and undressed

i am la cascarilla on the door, windows and vents
a protector of realms
i'm a bwiti shaman who ascends
i'm the mirror the root and the end

when the sun goes down

you better be wearing another
woman's scent, clothes disheveled
forget to zip your pants
sweaty palms
fidgeting through curtains
i watch the day turn over
and the twilight settle
so long as you walk through that door

i keep rockin between
the knob and the chair
testin my nerve
sittin and pacin
sittin again
the way my heart hoverin
this house haunted
boy you better be cheating on me
less i find you dead
it better be another woman

i called everyone three times too much
your cuzin went to the bar and knocked on all your brother's heads
till they was spinning one by one

in my living room
we checked the rivers for word
and asked the tire tracks had they seen your face
at least pretend to be alive
let a phone ring

any minute now
any minute
you gon walk
straight through that door
and lift me up like the sun

from eternity to eternity

we won't be the last to love
to lose or to mourn
for years we go on breaking or beating
what is within undoes what we were as we are
who emerges, who endures
never wait for who you will be to be who you are
no lie can undo a truth
whatever they say know you are worthy of listening

what journal does a bird or fish keep?
what tweet do leaves speak? current of stream, or falling of rain
who carries ocean's fury or tells
the story of its loss? the clouds' revenge?
what blog? what feed?

we are always dying, at best, we breathe
put your ear to the chest of words,
press your face against a voice
what is its heart? which way does its wind blow?
does it knock? lift or hold back?
what is any word that does not shiver the skin,
branches fluttering, turn a forest into wind chime
are we awake, alive even?

cells are rearranged by our bravery
the courage to see and question
a sound as a symbol of an inner ear
who hears the injured ant's tale?

barely crawling, lay your eye to the earth and listen
where it hurts, how it longs to move as it pleases, again
to be pleased
who will take a stand for the fallen ones?

cawing, chirp, cull or kill
no man will greet you like the sun's ray

there is no goodbye like parting with a moon
the joy of life is not given, it lives.
spirits do not lose nor do they win
our vision is low lit, lulled by keys and tones
in this season of storms, of rinsing and cures
those who do not bend will break
earth will not quiver over a deed to land
nor your right to shop and be photoshopped

earth knows nothing of politics
cares even less
earth is not in the business of forgiving
she is not in the business of business
she is burying her bitterness
laying her loved ones to rest
in the stillness of a well-aimed bullet
either you were spared or forced to repent
god is a bloody bartender
listening for the drip of a well-orchestrated spill
the mess of this dazzling maze
what song will we go to our grave singing?

what song
what song
what song

the living room

for daniel agnew

what we gon do about something we can't do nothing about?
to where do we go to whom do we speak
for why do we have to say goodbye
whisper me your ways with wind and worry me again
your face shining behind the computer screen
gentle as the sun sighs
you are not even here and i must tell you these things
your presence a poem sitting in the living room

i carry the last package you'll ever send me through the airport,
hugging the relic of you
your name stickered on the return address to me
what is this metaphor carrying you with me through
the gated halls of busy comings and goings

in the back room of the house i was a thousand wails of wound,
when i opened the door there you were, a brother
you offered a laugh, a documentary,
perhaps a seat to sit by and talk.

you listened and in the quiet corners of our living room
i told you things i didn't have the courage to tell the love of my life.

you held them close and we bolted visions i do not know what,
writings poems i'd rush into the living room
thirsty to share the crafting of poem
and even when you didn't want to,
you lowered the tv volume and listened to the juggled lines
growing into a poem.

those were the days we brothered and sistered each other alone together

everything touched by the past
lightning sitting at the edge of god's couch
the ocean of our window waving

this is the day to day we loved by
the dishes in the sink, the skillet on the stove and dried Alfredo sauce,
the roaches who never paid rent,
nudging your knee to lift your legs as i mopped between the days,
the nickles and dimes of electricity bills,
the smell of jackfruit smacking the air
a basket of bruised mangoes on the kitchen floor,
who would walk the dogs when Phil wasn't home?

before theresa and barney and cameron moved in,
it was all of us jetting through life reckless and free,
disorganized organizers
you leaving your clothes in the dryer again

you can call or not call i don't care just send a glimpse of your grin again
what i wouldn't give to tell you to not walk in the house with your shoes on

i was grieving before this grief and i did not know a heart could mope
this low in my chest, a drum-less circle, i was already missing you, brother
the tenderness of tragedy
where do messages go that were never sent?

i marvel at your tenacity
and i mourn not only for the loss of your brotherhood
but also for the self in me that is only known by you.
the intimate witnessing of my loving

in the end it was the things that drove me crazy about him that made me love him
isn't it always
it was the moments where we struggled and grew
with him and he grew with me.

the time is now
life is urgent
you moved urgently through life
the gifts that we have been given need to be utilized with the world
you were impeccable with your will to make something out of nothing

thank you, danny

i would choose this again and again
i would pour into you and reason and rage with your ruins
sifting the seance of our sayings

we debated the dreams we defended
the bond of being children turned adults too soon
bringing the parts of ourselves we loathed

we worked towards
we processed the presence of prayer
we did not always agree but it was the dimensions
of our deepening that lifted the values of our visions

i tattoo your memory on my arm
the hug the hold
the hell of losing you
a brother

i see you in the corners of my eye everywhere
the conversations of my memory
i will not lose you
you refuse to be lost
you are indeed, *pollen in the wild*
the weather in the wind
the tease in the tears
the laughter in the loneliness
you guard the house and make it a home

i remember you
spades on the front porch
modelo in your palm
chuckling at death
the revolution of our reckoning
a quiet boy spooning a pitbull like a long-lost friend
tender in your arms

the teddy bear of being a Black man
the soft silence of drifting
call it dreaming
what you did is what you've done
we built something
waiting by the window of dreams
every tale has a turn
Love was all there was
Love is all there is

in the brooklyn of our being

for chaddy chad

in the book of memory
your smile blossoms
dimples dance between us
and we eat each breath with our fingers
foodies for life

to friend
we walk the city streets with
the promise of pondering
sharing the shelter of sketched dreams
we chuckle at the rumors
of past lives
i will most miss the courage
of our conversations
tender strength facing the sunsets
of our sorrows
fumbling through photographs
of our hushed happiness
the creativity or your curiosity
sometimes we stared into the sky of awe
amazed at the evening of living
who will look out at the world with me
so wonderfully again?

the art of friending
the patience of your perspective
swag of your soft seeing
in the brooklyn of our being
we are both poets
our broken hearts widen
the boulevards of our kindness
sitting on the front stoop of selves
kickin it with the breeze

meet me in the book of memory
where the pages turn into portals
where forever is now
and sentences never end

i will miss the wisdom of your beginnings
the tall tales of our crushes
the brothering of your supportive brilliance

meet me in between chapters of silence
let us reminisce on the love of living
in the book of memory

you are the truest of friends
everything is beautiful
even our grief
we always have enough time
please, don't be a stranger

life vest

down here on the ground
you look up at a friend
a sky without borders
passport of recognition
you teleport through a phone call
or social media post
a speechless chapter
time writing itself
the business of surviving
some years you cannot transcribe
so you visit one another
eyes crumbling with the script of grins
you are a gate agent of who you were before
that relationship or job or kid
the grief of having to grow up
without the nearness of knowing
details, blessings, and burdens
the boat of bruises between you
there are no tombstones for time
you offer apologies
for all the flights you did not take

what does it mean to be considered?

after lockdown

looked after, thought of, tucked in, held
or wondered about, attended to, regarded as
deserving of want or need, never alone in arms
another belonging
a heart horizon wide, to friend
a ship with sails
harness the wind, lean and lay where a wound dreams
not a weapon or trigger to pull or peel
pain is a rattlesnake whispering sweet nothings of forever
the end gazing back at you
care is a voice with hands
trembling courage a hold letting go
here is a sip of love, warm and unspeakable music
opens a chest, clears a throat like herbal tea
homemade breath crossing lung to lung
sharing air like a kiss
soft cough drop soothing shame
like the rhythm of uncontrollable laughter
when you are sick it's the gentle gestures of grace
a song in the thick of grief
a lightened load of laundry
falling heavy on a shoulder
care is a room full of listening
care is familiar and thankless
while people hoard their nothingness
lounging in despair
the earth cleanses itself
of greed and cancer clinging to our bones
uncertainty rocks us to sleep
mouthing words of prayerless tomorrows
clutching pearls of market driven identity
work filled and empty
everyone's chasing shadows on a conference call or in an email
but care is knocking on your door

like abuelita waiting on line for food stamps
care has mouths to feed
wastes no words
is a deliberate cliché: *tomorrow's not promised*
the way the ground carries your feet is a care
or how the dishes don't wash themselves
care is inconvenient and intentional

like poetry pouring out anyway

what a poem is

today i will not be a metaphor you weigh all comparisons to
nor a simile you like as a hashtag
the only link we share is arms marching in a new direction
this is not a retweet that will ring in the doorbell of your palms
nor insecurities sweated with false promises

i know what a poem is.

this is not wordplay or flattery
i know what a poem is
this isn't a post-it note or lazy affirmation
this is not self-help sound bites
a poem is:
    what shivers and oozes sugared visions reflections of madness
    a moving target through clairvoyant eyes a spine made of spears
truth on its way a ripple in the pond
spirituals on spotlight spark like a bullet spitting back blood
this is not another would-be poem to tell you what you already want to hear
we suffer
a forest of lovers unfit and ashamed of flight

shoulders who forgot their wings
the audience must know applause fails all good things
this isn't a poem unless
you rise in the riots of words and do something
different today than yesterday
gems plucked from a blues song no shackles will shimmer here

it is another day another man weaves
his way into the hearts of many
little did we watch the music in his mother or the many
sisters who know what a poem is too
the work
the line break
the form
the stanza

how we bend into a sentence singing

brave words that have endured beyond sound
the humble tug of a wound revealed by secrets
that swim in moonlight
spoonfuls of scars say something different in morning
this is not a beggar's language
will not worry for others to claim our matter or mystery
a poem whispers love song chants and this pain
bless your face grinning in mine barefoot and dancing
the more we laugh the wiser we become
famous for nothing more than existing
we who always mattered before and after the phrase to affirm us was ever
    necessary

a poem is who you are when you forget your birth pains brought you into this
    earth
crying and still someone's tears showered you in welcomes and open arms
someone's prayers on maroon tongues conjured you
here now
it is too much fight and battle knuckle and lash endured
for us to turn back now,
to get on being comfortable and respected for the finer things
we do not age like wine
we age like wisdom
have you no heart
this country will sell you yours and claim
a percentage of all its earnings
part memories and part tomorrows

this is a poem
let us write a poem

the herbs that cured our aches
a spirit that jumps at the door of your body
the house of difference
when lies are the air we breathe

they are made of words
the poem is coded
comes like fresh water
there are many ways of being fed
this is food to nourish the person
society starves

wholesome and swole belly being
those who are hungry for cliches and shiny things
this is not for the weary
a poem creates a cosmos based on connection
is action
the common ground
a manifestation
the land we live on
though we felt buried
we were blooming
a poem for the poems that failed us.

atone
magical realist
time happened to us
we are the question of time itself
past present futures
all is as it was and will be
borderless imaginations
made of sound and vibes
the words are what we put love in
sip, drink, be fed, abundance is your bread
breathe   Blak   resist

supreme love

because their anger is not ours to carry
their bullets or brokenness
because hopeless is not our horizon
because healing is duty and obligation
because god is a holy action
a woman who changes with weather
because in between we dance
because times are hard and we are timeless
because we cherish the groove and ground we walk on water
and wishes well worn
because we suffer without defeat
refusing to be destroyed
because we miracle and magic
charm and spell
because we forgive but never forget
we know justice isn't determined by a judge
because karma never dies
for the wizards and ways of our defiance
visions of our rising risen selves
overcoming grace
firespitter tongues
wise as rickety rocking chairs
suffering salt and sand skies
memories unshackled
shining stitches on a stretch marked heart
for the flowers that bloom in midnight scars
how we suffered and sought a north star
when there was no light
we glowed and sparked
this rejoice this righteous delight
this reunion a longing to be held
the endless embrace
we got a cause to take joy in
how we weathered and persisted
tenacious
no stone unturned

moonlit laughter

patient smiles reminiscing on first times

mistakes and unrequited loves

playful and fresh

kinfolk codes of cool calm and copacetic

how we witnessed the horror of mankind and did not become that which
horrified us

a love s o   supreme.

say it with your chest

whatever touches your heart
feed fuel fight for it
flower heal hold
help have honor it
whatever touches your heart
promise hope hell and highwater
wade with it
shield protect keep it sacred
what ever
what
ever
ever what
whatever touches your heart
a future inevitable as hurt
let it wind through you
be fiercely undone
bold brave and bellowing
elbow ankle shoulder your way
will it as so
whatever
whatever it may be that fires
the engine of your chest
sprawls open your thoughts of you
unminded and moved
let it be
let it silly shame and show you out
remember when before memory
made you in the nameless nothing of now
let light lead you into the darling darkness
of not knowing
yet to know what it is to feel alive living
whatever
whatever it may be that touches your heart
that vibrating hungry heavy-handed heart
let it be luminous
unleash the firefly eager to be held

let it
let
let it be.

gratitude

i give thanks to the land of the Downstream people of Miami, Florida. to the cleansing ocean baths, mango and jackfruit trees, the sermon of dragonflies, blue jays, lizards, iguanas, the bougainvillea bush that framed our doorway before hurricane Irma's winds. to the free-spirted roosters of Little Haiti and their tiny hips thudding the streets. to the poems shaped as children in Liberty City and the Belafonte TACOLCY Center. to Legion Park Farmer's Market, Ms. Shirley, and the fresh sugar cane juice. to my beloved pit bulls, Smokey Baldwin & Melonius Miles, for showing me unconditional love and teaching me the responsibility of that love. shoving beside barbed wire to watch y'all run free in vacant lots beneath indigo mornings and bird of paradise evenings. i give thanks for friendship and fellowship. for front stoop conversations and conspiracies, living room television marathons, and kitchen confessionals. to 280 NW 46th street and all the love and community made between those walls.

to Daphne Kolader for patience, compassion, and faith in my obsession with metaphors and music. to Lauren Hill, my truest friend, healer, and keeper of secrets, a scrapbook of quilted memories shared between us. Naiomy Guerrero, my sister in heart and spirit, translator of orishas and oracles. to Meena Jagganath, a comrade, a visionary, and an artist pretending to be a lawyer. to Alana Greer, for your support of big ideas and your ever-extending heart of possibility. to the late and great Daniel Agnew, for being a brother and co-conspirator of imagination made real. and to Cameron Agnew, for baking zucchini chocolate bread on demand and helping me plant things in the home when no one else would. for being family. to Valencia Gunder, for your love of Miami and your gift of invitation. to Armen Henderson and his loving family for being present and always answering random calls about our health. the embodiment of a community-centered doctor. to Maria Arellano, for loving persistence, consistency, and rolling up your sleeves to help get the work done.

to Mohammed el-Kurd, for your sobering sense of humor and sacred feedback. Nelson Caban, for the years between us, the recurring laughter no matter how much time has passed. to Cameron Burkett and your beautiful eyes. thank you for seeing me. to Def Sound, for your honest love and the keeping of truth-telling bonds. to Novena Carmel, for the gift of your smiling hugs and the presence of your listening ears and heart. for treading with me through the cross-country transition. for your sistering. to Hollis Heath, for your loving compassion, brilliant sense of humor, and long-distance meme-sharing friendship. big enduring love to Derecka Purnell and Nyle Emerson for your encouraging supportive words and presence. for making me feel like an integral part of our vast movement for better lives.

i give thanks for the gift of community and the political education of dreaming with the Dream Defenders, Community Justice Project, ROOTS Collective, and BLCK Family. to Voices: Poetry for the People, we made incredible magic together; thank you for offering poems and making them real in our lives. i give thanks for mentorship, guidance, and support over the years. thank you to V (eve ensler) for guiding me through this phase of life as an artist and woman with treasured care and thoughtfulness. for offering an example of emotionally intelligent cultural work. for reading my poems and nurturing my inner most little girl self. to Mahogany L. Browne for pouring into me, lifting me up, and helping me raise my visions of being a poet into a flourishing reality. for bearing witness all these many years. for being in my corner and helping me edit this book into a vision of my own making. i love you.

thank you to Anthony Arnove and the Haymarket Books team for supporting the publication of my poems in the world. thank you to Charlotte Sheedy and Jesseca Salky for believing in my work at this time, of all times.

there are many days i wanted to give up on poetry, on life, on publishing at all. and so, i give thanks to, you, reader. thank you for spending time with these words and for continuing to attend readings where i get to share these poems aloud. for caring. for returning to my work so that it may continue to be a part of your journey.

about the author

aja monet is a surrealist blues poet, musician, and cultural worker whose poems sing to us of love, gender, justice, and spirituality. A graduate of Sarah Lawrence College and the School of the Art Institute of Chicago, her writing sways between realms where the poetic is both a prayer and a call to action.

Her debut poetry collection, *My Mother Was a Freedom Fighter*, a tribute to women and girls in the pursuit of freedom, earned a 2018 NAACP Image Award nomination for poetry. In 2023, she released *When the Poems Do What They Do*, a debut album of jazz and blues poetry. In 2024, she earned a Grammy nomination for Best Spoken Word Poetry Album, a testament to her voice, both on the page and in the world.

As artistic creative director for the *Voices: A Scared Sisterscape* audioplay and campaign with V-Day, monet is part of the global movement to end violence against women and girls. monet is a recipient of the EBONY Power 100 Artist in Residence Award, Tribeca Film Festival's Harry Belafonte Social Justice Award, and the Nelson Mandela Changemaker Award.

about Haymarket Books

Haymarket Books is a radical, independent, nonprofit book publisher based in Chicago. Our mission is to publish books that contribute to struggles for social and economic justice. We strive to make our books a vibrant and organic part of social movements and the education and development of a critical, engaged, and internationalist Left.

We take inspiration and courage from our namesakes, the Haymarket Martyrs, who gave their lives fighting for a better world. Their 1886 struggle for the eight-hour day—which gave us May Day, the International Workers' holiday—reminds workers around the world that ordinary people can organize and struggle for their own liberation. These struggles—against oppression, exploitation, environmental devastation, and war—continue today across the globe.

Since our founding in 2001, Haymarket has published more than nine hundred titles. Radically independent, we seek to drive a wedge into the risk-averse world of corporate book publishing. Our authors include Angela Y. Davis, Arundhati Roy, Keeanga-Yamahtta Taylor, Eve L. Ewing, aja monet, Mariame Kaba, Naomi Klein, Rebecca Solnit, Olúfẹ́mi O. Táíwò, Mohammed el-Kurd, José Olivarez, Noam Chomsky, Winona LaDuke, Robyn Maynard, Leanne Betasamosake Simpson, Howard Zinn, Mike Davis, Marc Lamont Hill, Dave Zirin, Astra Taylor, and Amy Goodman, among many other leading writers of our time. We are also the trade publishers of the acclaimed Historical Materialism Book Series. Haymarket also manages a vibrant community organizing and event space in Chicago, Haymarket House, the popular Haymarket Books Live event series and podcast, and the annual Socialism Conference.

also by Haymarket Books

All the Blood Involved in Love, Maya Marshall

Ankle-Deep in Pacific Water, E. Hughes

Build Yourself a Boat, Camonghne Felix

Citizen Illegal, José Olivarez

I Remember Death by Its Proximity to What I Love, Mahogany L. Browne

Like a Hammer: Poets on Mass Incarceration, edited by Diana Marie Delgado

A Map of My Want, Faylita Hicks

My Mother Was a Freedom Fighter, aja monet

Nazar Boy, Tarik Dobbs

O Body, Dan "Sully" Sullivan

Rifqa, Mohammed El-Kurd

Super Sad Black Girl, Diamond Sharp

There Are Trans People Here, H. Melt

Too Much Midnight, Krista Franklin

We the Gathered Heat: Asian American and Pacific Islander Poetry, Performance, and Spoken Word, edited by Franny Choi, Bao Phi, Noʻu Revilla, and Terisa Siagatonu